PAINTING
RAIN

PAULA MEEHAN

PAINTING RAIN

 Wake Forest University Press

Wake Forest University Press

Published simultaneously in paperback
and in a clothbound edition.
First North American edition published 2009

Wake Forest University Press
Post Office Box 7333
Winston-Salem, NC 27109

Cover design by Jessica Koman
Printed on Acid-free, recycled paper
in the United States of America

Library of Congress Catalogue Number 2008943053
ISBN 978-1-930630-42-0 (paperback)
ISBN 978-1-930630-43-7 (clothbound)

First published in the U.K. by Carcanet Press

2nd printing

wfupress.wfu.edu

for Eavan Boland

Words cannot express Truth.
That which words express is not Truth.
The Diamond Sutra

The mysteries of the forest disappear with the forest.
Theo Dorgan

Contents

Death of a Field

The field itself is lost the morning it becomes a site
When the Notice goes up: Fingal County Council – 44 houses

The memory of the field is lost with the loss of its herbs

Though the woodpigeons in the willow
The finches in what's left of the hawthorn hedge
And the wagtail in the elder
Sing on their hungry summer song

The magpies sound like flying castanets

And the memory of the field disappears with its flora:
Who can know the yearning of yarrow
Or the plight of the scarlet pimpernel
Whose true colour is orange?

The end of the field is the end of the hidey holes
Where first smokes, first tokes, first gropes
Were had to the scentless mayweed

The end of the field as we know it is the start of the estate
The site to be planted with houses each two- or three-bedroom
Nest of sorrow and chemical, cargo of joy

The end of dandelion is the start of Flash
The end of dock is the start of Pledge
The end of teazel is the start of Ariel
The end of primrose is the start of Brillo
The end of thistle is the start of Bounce
The end of sloe is the start of Oxyaction
The end of herb robert is the start of Brasso
The end of eyebright is the start of Persil

Who amongst us is able to number the end of grasses
To number the losses of each seeding head?

                                    I'll walk out once
Barefoot under the moon to know the field
Through the soles of my feet to hear
The myriad leaf lives green and singing
The million million cycles of being in wing

That – before the field become map memory
In some archive on some architect's screen
I might possess it or it possess me
Through its night dew, its moon-white caul
Its slick and shine and its profligacy
In every wingbeat in every beat of time

Not Weeding

Nettle, bramble, shepherd's purse –
refugees from the building site
that was once the back field,

my former sworn enemies
these emissaries of the wild
now cherished guests.

Tanka

When he stepped ashore
his eyes were the deepest green
as if he dreamt leaves
across the wide Atlantic
to reel him home to Ireland.

Opening his book
I wrote – the wake of bristle
barely dipped in ink
that brushed on dampened paper,
invites a poem pool to light

through the pulse beating
wane of the moon, as land ebbs
from him, the tide line
washing clean the page's span,
making fast the boat – the stars

that brought him back safe
shine further into night skies
wheeling overhead
in a new constellation
less finned nor furred than feathered.

This coming winter
he will dream the vast ocean
back into his eyes.
The morning he'll rise to leave
his eyes will be deepest blue.

Deadwood

Me with the secateurs, you with the Greek saw;
we cut the creeper back, we prune the rose;
cotoneaster and privet get the chop –
more on the compost heap than left on hedge.

The walls look cold, naked; the shrubbery raw
and wounded where we snip. We trust it grows
back. You're stuck up the ladder reaching to lop
off a cankerous branch. Your tool's honed edge

whines as it goes. All day you lay down the law.
You'd swear you'd a PhD in pruning. God knows
I'm as bad with my cranks and my post op
critique of your handiwork; or worse – I dredge

from our primeval bed, the sea's wide floor,
my pearls of wisdom, my swinish garden lore.

At Dublin Zoo

A four-year-old
Seeing elephants
For the first time

'But they're not blue'

On Howth Head

In May,
Bealtaine, Beltane, Baal's Fire

the flaming gorse
dropping blossom to stone

remembering Theo beside me
last autumn a hot day

when each gorse pod cast seed
in myriad explosions all over the head

the extent of the transmission
blazing out now.

'She didn't know she was dying but the poems did'

for Jody Allen Randolph

She didn't know she was dying but the poems did.
They carried on as usual. They understood

that every moon was a waning moon,
each flower already past its bloom;

the city of her birth was a ghost city,
even the ghosts had exhausted her pity;

her old lovers, her mother, her lost children
were muddled into the ghost cauldron.

When she got Lough Léinn in a line
it was for the toxic algal scum, the greenish-brown

stain spreading over the surface of water
by whose shores Oisín had hunted deer

through the *ceo draíochta* that presaged Niamh.
The old language itself was a reason to grieve.

So many dying languages. Her ode to the Nushu tongue
of Central China, the last woman-specific language

as far as she could tell, which died with Yang Huanji
of Hunan Province, in her 98th year, could be

read as foreshadowing her own death.
Certainly the lines shortened, as if breath

itself was thinning, ornament sparse,
the poem a horse-drawn vehicle, a hearse

clipping along, not as in wild youth the thunderous ride
bare-back, white-knuckled above the thundering tide.

The poems kept the secret of her death from her:
when the mooring line went slack in the water,

and her craft began its slow drift into the light –
rudderless, the shrouds no longer taut

to the truck, the clouds a raggy flag atop the mast.
She was free to go with the current at last.

Her death belonged to the poems; they kept it
safe from her, knowing she would not accept it.

Hagiography

Just back from Éigse Michael Hartnett.
You'd have to laugh. His corpse not even cold yet.

Very aboriginal to be beneath a sign at the brand new estate:
Address – Michael Hartnett Close, Newcastle West.

Its position is perfect – right opposite Coole Lane.
Stood there in the pouring rain with his son

Across from The Healing Streams Therapy Centre,
St Vincent de Paul, within earshot of the river

On a quiet day.
                        Get this: the story Joan MacKernan
Told us of the poetry workshop for children

Earlier, when she asked who'd heard of Michael Hartnett,
The lad who cried 'Miss, Miss, I live in Michael Hartnett.'

I recognised the mantra
Like a glittering speck of mica

Whirling down the bardos from another incarnation
To blaze the words as the tune is spun.

All together now: I live in Michael Hartnett.
I live in Michael Hartnett. I live in Michael Hartnett.

The Following Message Will Be Deleted From Your Mailbox

message ... from ... an ... unidentified ... source ...

And then your next breath. Your next to, next to, next to, next to –
how many next to's exactly? – next to last breath.

Your last phone call. Which I wasn't there to answer.
So the last breath of yours I'd ever hear. Or half
a breath rather. The intake. Not the exhale.

And then nothing. A rustle. Paper? Hard as I listen
I cannot be sure. I'm setting the scene
after your cup of tea and your smokes running low,

after you tidy your room, after you cue the CDs,
after you write the notes. The general all purpose note
and the short notes with private farewells. After

you write the cards, the birthday cards for those of us
with birthdays coming soon (have a lovely time
on your special day – yeah thanks a bunch),

after you lock the door and deadbolt it,
after you draw the blinds on the late light of summer.
Or maybe before. Before your cup of tea

and your smokes running low, before you tidy the room,
before you decide on the tunes, before the notes and the cards,
the blighted cards, before you draw the blinds

on summer forever, you called me up and left your breath.
Breath I listened to again and again and again
days after you were ash on the tide, turned in the tide's wide arms.

A week to the moment you sent it – *the following message
will be deleted ...* – gone with the static of wires,
held fast in memory until my own breath fails.

Sea

for Tony Walsh

From Scratch

To begin again: my hands sifting sand
at the sea's edge, and nothing to be done.
All day to do it in. To start again
from scratch; a driftwood stick, a hazel wand
to scribe your name deep in the newfound land
the ebbing tide has granted me. The sun
is a time bomb tossed to the blue heaven;
clouds shadow my script, shadow my young hand.
A heron takes flight as if not knowing
yet what its own wings can do. There are reams
of brent geese landing with their hungry song.
At the tide's edge your name – going, going
gone with the turning tide. What was mere dream
of empire – dissolved, wrecked. Gone badly wrong.

High Tide

When we stole out of the sleeping estate
down to the sea shore, we were thieves of night.
We were thieves of grief, of longing, of light.
Hand in hand, each the other's chosen mate.

We wanted to copperfasten our fate
in the sound of, in the face of, in sight
of, the highest tide either one of us might
know. We wanted to feel that mortal weight.

The neighbours must have shifted in their dreams
and turned, or sighed, or called out of their sleep
some lost love's name, some unmourned daughter's death;
as in: my Sarah, my Nancy, my Liam.
Lyric of their secret fret the sea keeps –
the drowned forever singing their last breath.

Sullen

The islands appear, they vanish, return.
        A dog worries her image in a pool;
disturbs the mirror, digs deep in the sand,
        self unfathomable. And I, who learn
this craft at the expense of art: mere fool
        that the sea abandons high on dry land.

Handsel

I take my black dog down to the winter sea;
a mere drop in the ocean each salt tear.
The north wind is bitter, threatening snow;
it whips up the waves, it whines through the dunes.
A small boat is wrecked on the rocks – dragged free
of its mooring, dismasted, all its gear
and tackle cast on the tide. A lone crow
blown from the woods caws his hooded tune
to the water.
        O the sea neither gives
nor takes as we fancy. The sea has no needs,
nor worries, nor wants. If we call it 'she' –
an ur-mother – it is because salt lives
in our blood. And grief drops salt like seeds;
brings home shells in pockets – memory.

Ashes

The tide comes in; the tide goes out again
washing the beach clear of what the storm
dumped. Where there were rocks, today there is sand;
where sand yesterday, now uncovered rocks.

So I think on where her mortal remains
might reach landfall in their transmuted forms,
a year now since I cast them from my hand
– wanting to stop the inexorable clock.

She who died by her own hand cannot know
the simple love I have for what she left
behind. I could not save her. I could not
even try. I watch the way the wind blows
life into slack sail: the stress of warp against weft
lifts the stalling craft, pushes it on out.

Nomad Heart

for Kevin Page

Sometimes looking to the cold wintry stars
you can feel the planet move as it whirls
in the flux of the galaxy, the whole
path of the milky way buzzing like a hive.

They say it's better to journey than arrive –
halting being the usual rigmarole
of move-along-shift. Sometimes the soul
just craves a place to rest, safe from earthly wars.

The city lights come on in twos and threes
and leaves are freezing hard in mucky pools,
cars are stuck in jams or droning home.

If we're not brought to our knees, we'll fall to our knees
in thanks, in praise, in trust, in hope – the rule
of law mapped clear on heaven's ample dome.

Six Sycamores

The original leaseholders around St Stephen's Green had to plant six sycamores and tend them for three years.

The Sycamore's Contract with the Citizens

To look up in autumn – the fiery crown
loosing and netting the sky by turns; the seeds
stopping time, helicoptering lazily down
to crashland on paths or on a pad of weeds

when you were a child. And imagined the birds
as the souls of the builders; their flighty shades
gossip through the years' unleaving – their words
drift slowly down the airwaves as the light fades.

To remember the planters with their common tools,
spade, rake, hoe; the forms so crafty, so good,
so sharp, so meet for the job, nobody fool
enough to try to improve on them. Dream of bud;

and earth's opening gesture to the root of the sycamore
as it probes below ground for the source of this metaphor.

09.20   First Sycamore

a girl stops for a moment
a stone in her boot
on her Walkman Bob Dylan
he that's not busy being born is busy dying
she's late for school
she smokes a last fag

Number Fifty-One

And as the ages pass, the solid world longs
for its own dissolution: those red bricks
dream of the clay pit; with every lick
of the north wind rough render remembers the song

of the river grinding it down; granite quoins desire
their home in the mountains – above Ballyknockan, the wild
bird's lonely tune, the shadow on the lake;

the iron railings guard the memory of fire,
of ore-selves before being smelted and cast and exiled
to these unforgiving streets; the shutters ache

for the woods, the greeny light, the sap strong
in bole, in branch, the undergrowth quick
with life; linen drapes must crave someone to unpick,
to unspin, to be bluest flax blossom all summer long.

04.26   Second Sycamore

you couldn't take your eyes off of her
give us a break
you were looking at her all night
for the love and honour …
you don't care about me
will you shush
you don't give a toss
you'll wake the dead
you were drooling over her
donne moi un break wagon
come back here you

Number Fifty-Two

La Touche is in his counting house, counting out
his money. He's piling up the gold coin
in neat and shiny rows. A twinge of gout
but otherwise all well. The new house on the Green

is splendid, plasterwork sublime, furnishings divine
and Angelica Kauffmann turning up on a chance
visit. Such a boon. He'll hurry to join
her for tea before dark. He can already sense

her copy of Guido's *Aurora* is a work of immense
beauty. The way she's found in the pearly light
of a Dublin dawn the exact tone for the dance
of all that mythic flesh across his ceiling. She might

well paint the grove's tender green from those sycamores.
She's worth her weight in snotty stuccodores!

12.53   Third Sycamore

spare a few bob mister
a few bob for a cup of tea
any odds mister
spare change please
help the homeless missus
a few pence for a hostel
god bless you love
spare a few bob mister

'all trades, their gear and tackle and trim'
Father Hopkins

Their kit and their rig. The beloved adze and auger,
bodkin and borer, chisel and clamp, diestock and drill,
the edgetools and files, graver, hammer, inker,
the jemmy, knives, lathe and mitre, the mill,

the nibbler; on and on in serried ranks,
the marching army of the wielders of tools.
And whether they are saints or fools
we'll raise a glass and offer thanks

to the makers and minders of our material world.
In their war against time: daemons fire them;
St Joseph bear them; muses inspire them.
Guild banner, lodge pennant, red flag of labour unfurled!

And somewhere in the upper story the Architect
uncertain whether to dance or genuflect.

14.48   Fourth Sycamore

she feels a kick in her belly
on her way to Holles Street
for the seven-month checkup
she steadies herself at the tree
imagining the rings within the bark
she waits for her creature to settle
her first child

Them Ducks Died for Ireland

'6 of our waterfowl were killed or shot, 7 of the garden seats broken and
about 300 shrubs destroyed.'
Park Superintendent in his report on the damage to
St Stephen's Green, during the Easter Rising 1916

Time slides slowly down the sash window
puddling in light on oaken boards. The Green
is a great lung, exhaling like breath on the pane
the seasons' turn, sunset and moonset, the ebb and flow

of stars. And once made mirror to smoke and fire,
a Republic's destiny in a Countess' stride,
the bloodprice both summons and antidote to pride.
When we've licked the wounds of history, wounds of war,

we'll salute the stretcher-bearer, the nurse in white,
the ones who pick up the pieces, who endure,
who live at the edge, and die there and are known

by this archival footnote read by fading light;
fragile as a breathmark on the windowpane or the gesture
of commemorating heroes in bronze and stone.

06.17   Fifth Sycamore

coming off the nightshift
the youth dreams of the Lotto
they can all fuck off then
the McBoss with his McJob
with his McMobile and his McMind
from the airport he'll text them
I resign

Liminal

I've always loved thresholds, the stepping over,
the shapechanging that can happen when
you jump off the edge into pure breath and then
the passage between inner and outer.

Mist becomes cloud; becomes rain. Water. Ice. Water.
In the daily flux, no telling where one will end or begin.
Death can kick start and birth be the true El Fin.
You jig and you reel through molecular spin, daughter.

Nothing can harm you or cure you. You've found
a clear path through the chaos, a loaning

from history and whether you are free or bound
is still in the balance. There's no gain in owning.

Old riddles still posit the same – what is the sound
of one hand clapping? Is that the door opening or closing?

19.38   Sixth Sycamore

years later he tells her
he hid behind the tree
and watched her
sitting on granite steps
waiting for him to show
their first date
spring blossom falling like snow

Her Void: A Cemetery Poem

Those lips that once reached thirsty
for the breast, not silted now with milk
but all stopped up with dust.

Her mouth that pursed in anger at a slight
or puckered for a kiss, that sulked then broke
into a smile – is now a rictus grin.

She might have made orisons to star, planet, moon,
or to the god she learnt her prayers for,
but now she's dumb, her world unpraised.

She'll speak no bitter word, no curse
or twisted cleverality; no slight, no mean sarcasm
will riffle the calm pool of her void.

The whirr of a bee's wing is music for her
and the rosined bow of the cricket,
and sad percussive raindrops.

Her song is the wind in the branches
the small bird feathering her nest.
Rest here weary pilgrim;
sit and take a breath.

In Memory, Joanne Breen

I am fingering a length of yarn
from the mill at Stornoway.
It is green as a summer meadow
though when I untwine it widdershins
I see, spun into the yarn, fibres of blue
& yellow & purple, occasionally orange.

I am undoing the magic of the spindle,
Unravelling.

The day we buried her, gorse was a golden flame.

We buried the summer with her, we buried
high clouds of May, the swallows we buried –
those stitchers of land to sea, those grafters of sky
to the dark earth which opened to her beauty.

We buried the song of her body and all it promised
of betrothal & children & work: the way
she would weave dolphin & salmon & swan
in a tapestry out of the land itself,
its very warp & woof, its stuff, its dye, its fixings,
the land she trod so lightly on.

I am fingering a length of yarn
from the mill at Stornoway. Deep winter now
and the wind crying in the chimney.
The candle gutters in a draught;
the shadow sways on the wall
and breath – breath snags on memory.

Once upon a springtime she is a girl
in the branches of an old beech in the back field.
She holds fast to the rope and out she jumps –

the dog, the clouds, the hedgerows,
the rooftop, the haybarn, the cows,
the stream, the starlings, the byre,
the bees, the hill, the village,
all spun together – dizzy and giddy she laughs
swinging out into the arms of our love.

Snowdrops

So long trying to paint them, failing
to paint their shadows on the concrete path.

They are less a white than a bleaching out of green.
If you go down on your knees

and tilt their petals towards you
you'll look up under their petticoats

into a hoard of gold
like secret sunlight and their

three tiny striped green awnings that lend a
kind of frantic small-scale festive air.

It is the first day of February
and I nearly picked a bunch for you,

my dying friend, but remembered in time
how you prefer to leave them

to wither back into the earth;
how you tell me it strengthens the stock.

Cora, Auntie

Staring Death down
with a bottle of morphine in one hand,
a bottle of Jameson in the other:

laughing at Death –
love unconditional keeping her just this side
of the threshold

as her body withered
and her eyes grew darker and stranger
as her hair grew back after chemo

thick and curly as when she was a girl;
always a girl in her glance
teasing Death – humour a lance

she tilted at Death.
Scourge of Croydon tram drivers and High Street dossers
on her motorised invalid scooter

that last year:
bearing the pain,
not crucifixion but glory

in her voice.
Old skin, bag of bones,
grinning back at the rictus of Death:

always a girl in her name –
Cora, maiden, from the Greek Κορη,
promising blossom, summer, the scent of thyme.

*

Sequin: she is standing on the kitchen table.
She is nearly twenty-one.
It is nineteen sixty-one.

They are sewing red sequins, the women,
to the hem of her white satin dress
as she moves slowly round and round.

Sequins red as berries,
red as the lips of maidens,
red as blood on the snow

in Child's old ballads,
as red as this pen
on this white paper

I've snatched from the chaos
to cast these lines
at my own kitchen table –

Cora, Marie, Jacinta, my aunties,
Helena, my mother, Mary, my grandmother –
the light of those stars

only reaching me now.
I orbit the table I can barely see over.
I am under it singing.

She was weeks from taking the boat to England.
Dust on the mantlepiece,
dust on the cards she left behind:

a black cat swinging in a silver horseshoe,
a giant key to the door,
emblems of luck, of access.

★

All that year I hunted sequins:
roaming the house I found them
in cracks and crannies,

in the pillowcase,
under the stairs,
in a hole in the lino,

in a split in the sofa,
in a tear in the armchair
in the home of the shy mouse.

With odd beads and single earrings,
a broken charm bracelet, a glittering pin,
I gathered them into a tin box

which I open now in memory –
the coinage, the sudden glamour
of an emigrant soul.

Peter, Uncle

I

Think memory a river.

Back then,
as far back as I can go,
near the headwaters:

a wind tossed a seed head in
and it is carried by the current
to this muddy shore

low lying estuarial land
of Baldoyle, part gravel bank
part coastal meadow
where I reach my fiftieth year

it snags and roots and grows and blossoms
now this flowering:

back then as far
back as I can go –

1961, '62? How old am I?
Six? Seven?

Me at the front of the scooter
standing between his knees
holding on for dear life.

Pat, my aunt, his wife-to-be, on the back,
off each Sunday after lunch
to look at how their house was growing

course by breezeblock course
in a field in Artane,
the city pushing out a new suburb.

The curiousness
to the solemn child I was
of Peter Field visiting a field where

he was like some god of the field,
hermetic of the thing and its name
and the blade cutting into the turf
to open the field
to let his will be done.

The house foundations were planted like crops in their neat rows
the song of cement mixers
brickies whistling in the winter air
the field itself dying as the crop matured.

That moment
when the roof went on –
what was enclosed then:
call that mystery home.

II

Forward: another memory
washes downriver to this estuarial backwater
for my gaze to fall on it –

me at thirteen in their kitchen,
children around us.

Peter drawing on the ember of his pipe –

*Look: this is how you change a fuse
are you paying attention?*

He explains the flow of it –

current   danger   you should know   you need to know

Who in those days would teach a girl such a thing?
Access, suddenly, knowledge.

III

He never gave up on me:
the family joke I became then –

pauper-poet, wandering star,
what is all this education for?
Down at heel and
down at mouth and
all prickles and class anger and
always in trouble and heartbroke,
what I remember of the 70s.

He never gave up on me.

IV

A night of rain,
such rain gurgling in the gutters
weeping in the shores
great struggling gulps of it against the rooves
sighing down the windowpanes

visiting the house end of the 90s
millennium looming and all that feverish excess

his bald head on the pillow
after chemo –

Buddhist monk, baby, camp inmate.
He is sleeping.

I turn away quickly from that door into the room
that once was air above a green field
summer stitched through it by swallows' deft needlework

I turn away from that memory
coming down with the floodwaters

coming down on city and suburb alike.

V

Walking the riverbank early spring
I come upon a clean pool
deep and still and mirroring
each star, the new moon,
and my own shadowy face.

An epic for days, for long nights:
each breath he fought for and won.

After the hospital and his last breath
I walk out to the river;

always the river pulling down to the sea.

His last gift,
his last breath –
ripple on the pool
ripples out forever;

I watch him take it –
my first death.
My own breath on the mirror
rising mist on the river.

Hannah, Grandmother

for Hannah McCabe

Coldest day yet of November
her voice close in my ear –

Tell them priests nothing.

Was I twelve? Thirteen?

Filthy minded.

Keep your sins to yourself.

Don't be giving them a thrill.

Dirty oul feckers.

As close as she came to the birds and the bees
on her knees in front of the Madonna,
Our Lady of the Facts of Life

beside the confessional –
oak door closing like a coffin lid

neatly carpentered
waxed and buffed.

In the well-made box of this poem
her voice dies.

She closes her eyes

and lowers her brow to her joined hands.
Prays hard:

woman to woman.

A Remembrance of my Grandfather, Wattie, Who Taught Me to Read and Write

for Seamus Heaney

Heading towards the Natural History Museum
across the snowy paths of Merrion Square
the city hushed, the park deserted, in a daydream
I look up: a heaving net of branches, leaf-bare
against the pearly sky. There, like a trireme
on an opalescent ocean, or some creature of the upper air
come down to nest, a cargo with a forest meme,
only begotten of gall, of pulp, of page, of leaflight, of feather.
What snagged that book in the high reaches of the oak?
A child let out of school, casting heavenward the dreary yoke?
An eco-installation from an artist of the avant-garde?
Or the book's own deep need to be with kindred –
a rootling cradled again in grandfather's arms,
freed of her history, her spells, her runes, her fading charms?

Prayer for the Children of Longing

*A poem commissioned by the community of Dublin's north inner city for the
lighting of the Christmas tree in Buckingham Street, to remember their
children who died from drug use.*

Great tree from the far northern forest
Still rich with the sap of the forest
Here at the heart of winter
Here at the heart of the city

Grant us the clarity of ice
The comfort of snow
The cool memory of trees
Grant us the forest's silence
The snow's breathless quiet

For one moment to freeze
The scream, the siren, the knock on the door
The needle in its track
The knife in the back

In that silence let us hear
The song of the children of longing
In that silence let us catch
The breath of the children of longing

The echo of their voices through the city streets
The streets that defeated them
That brought them to their knees
The streets that couldn't shelter them
That spellbound them in alleyways
The streets that blew their minds
That led them astray, out of reach of our saving
The streets that gave them visions and dreams
That promised them everything
That delivered nothing

The streets that broke their backs
The streets that we brought them home to

Let their names be the wind through the branches
Let their names be the song of the river
Let their names be the holiest prayers

Under the starlight, under the moonlight
In the light of this tree

Here at the heart of winter
Here at the heart of the city

The Age of Reason

A garden, a privet hedge, the smell of fresh concrete.
A newly dug flower bed

is a black crescent moon

on a green sky.

My Grandmother Mary
is picking lilac and roses to place on her May altar.

I think grace looks like the mother-of-pearl cover
on my eucharistic prayerbook.

Later a broken window, raised voices, my uncle
out of his head; all of us

sleeping in my auntie's bed.

Bad Fairy

The night of her christening:
the music blared, the cars and vans roared,
horns, sirens, beats,
all night, nobody could sleep.

There was a stabbing and a window got broken.
A car scratched with a key. One boy
got a bottle in the face
and someone puked in the garden.

I think of that now passing her house.
She must be all of nine
her face a shy moon
behind the twitching blind.

First Blood

A shadow cast by the clotheshorse onto the flickering wall.
heat of the fire, smell of scorched cotton.

Smoke, flame, alarm. Someone, my mother,
throwing the sheet into the fire.

My first sight of blood, her hand ripped on the fireguard.

Always after
a horse, a rider, a pointy-nosed devil,
riding the picture rail, the ceiling, the wardrobe,

coming to get us with fire, with blood.

When I Was a Girl

I longed for a boat
a hollowed log
seabirds carved its length
to fly it through the waves
of bleached white nappies in their rows

line after line
wave after wave
some sad celebration

for my setting forth

looking down on them through the big
window

Seán McDermott Street

22E Upper.

Shoes

The day I gave you back your death
I pulled off my winter boots.

Washed them. Waxed them. Polished them
Until I could see my shorn head

Grin back at me.
And though it was late November

And the snow was sifting quietly into drifts
In the pure light of the moon

I put on your summer shoes.
They smelt of the red red earth

Where lemons grow, where olives grow.
I walked away from the house.

The door swung shut behind me.

A Stray Dream

It's a happy dream though in it you were
Humping some dancer in a run-down gaff

A seafront hotel out of season where
I'm in a kitchen on a single bed

I've pulled from a drawer like the silk scarf
Of the carny man who's filling in for

ManDuck the Magician star of stage and screen
I saw earlier that day at the end of the pier

I had sheets of Belfast linen but you
Had the dancer. And had her again

While the dawn struggled to break on the sea
And break on the quick and the slow and the dead

When I woke the next morning under the bed
Dustdevils, feathers and some child's brown shoes

Kippe

Like a knitted Dutch mitten
found in a patch of snow

I pull the word for little house
over my frozen fingers –

crawling in sunlight
over my own shadow

dragging my bundle of hides
my bundle of skins

towards the door and in
to the stink of sleep

my hand thawed at last
from its carapace of ice.

Old Skin

staggering towards me
I've cast you off

years ago
shrugged you off

left you, put you down at the side of the road
for ravening

by any passing predator
old skin – when your face splits open

in recognition –
you know me now

but not what bar you left me in –
what else would you say but

'how're ya, me old skin?'

Quitting the Bars

Quitting's hard but staying sober's harder.
The day by day; the drudge and boredom bit;
not sure if the self is cell or warder.

You quit the bars; you quit the sordid ardour;
you quit the tulpas sucking on your tit.
Quitting's hard but staying sober's harder.

You sometimes think you got away with murder.
The shady souls regard you as you sit —
you wonder if they are wards or warders

in this sad café. The mind's last border
dissolves. Guilt has done a midnight flit.
Quitting's hard but staying sober's harder.

So sip cool water; the light's a wonder
streaming out in wave-particles. You've lit
up bright your prison cell. Body — warder

of your dreams — will be the dreams' recorder,
though wrapped now in a skin that doesn't fit.
Quitting's hard but staying sober's harder;
stranger for your being both ward and warder.

Note from the Puzzle Factory

I went to the limit on Visa.
Bought eight and a half grand's worth
of mobiles, couriered them direct
to all my friends, here in the city
and down the country,
so they could keep in touch
day or night. With me.

Nobody rang. Nobody rang.
Imagine. Not a soul. Not a sinner.
I sat in my room thinking on this.
Then I up and signed myself in.

Who'd Be a Dog?

Who'd be a dog, who'd be a poet's dog?
When we could be up the beach digging holes
sniffing holes, cooling the paws in the sea,

she's stuck to her iBook, worrying a line
'stars so clear have been dead for years ...
stars so dead have been clear for years ...'
She thinks she's it with her buttons, her plug.

It's bye-bye puppy, hello Microsoft Word;
it's laptop now where once it was lapdog.

We look so cosy, me curled at her toes,
the two of us here in the house on our own.
If she dropped down dead this instant who'd know?
Who's a good doggy then, eh? Who's the best girl?

Give or take a day or two, it'd be a week max,
before, craven with hunger, I'd start in to eat:

top o' the foodchain to you, my last mistress!
as I lick at her bare, her coolèd feet.

Valentine

My sister phones to tell me that she found
when stripping old wallpaper from the hall
in thick black marker writ my name —
paula meehan kiss kiss love love — then yours,

enclosed within a heart. An arrow. The ground
shifts. I'd forgotten all that. I can call
to mind my nineteenth year with ease — the hames
we made of the job, woodchip (rough as furze

on the hands) overpainted green, the sound
of Dylan in mono, the rise and the fall
of your breath as you came and you went and you came,
as you did and you didn't, first mine, then hers,

then mine again. Never again. I'd sooner eat my
words, the wall they're written on. I'd sooner die.

Teaching 'Kubla Khan' to the FÁS Trainees at the Recovery through Art, Drama, and Education Project

for Gerald Dawe

They are most interested in the parts
of Coleridge's notebooks where he writes
of *acrimony of the bowels*

for he was a martyr to the constipation
as a side effect of opiate use and they
of course would recognise the symptoms,
one of the perils of heroin addiction.

So he was full of shite!
Like all yous poets.
Full of it. Full of yourselves.
That's what they mean by writer's block.
I wonder what he got off of the man from Porlock.
Knock knock me hole is blocked!

We are soon in high merriment
all twenty of us sitting in a circle
bags of shite, bags of bones

laughing our heads off
our clear and detoxed heads.

A Change of Life

real danger. gambles. and the edge of death.

from Gary Snyder,
'What You Should Know to be a Poet'

Prayer Before Starting

Let me just be
poised as that raindrop
on the tip of the tansy leaf
to freefall
to the earth below.

The Book of Changes

is best read by starlight
with plenty of time on your hands –
glint of coin, sheen of yarrow.

Elemental now, or mental
my two feet solid on this earth –
the path ahead, the path behind.

Not a question of which way to turn:
more a question of when to move –
the earth in its devotion carries all things

Scrying

The stars have a purple glow and the red
devil of desire is jerking our strings:
we are avid puppets in his hands.

Enslaved by money and the lure of power
we rattle our talismans. Our dance,
if we have one anymore, is under

the baton of St Vitus, millennial, macabre.
This new fever has a grip on the island
and everyone wants, wants, wants

more space, more grace, more avoirdupois
wandering around with our lower material selves
hanging out – like that boy the other day

near the dying chestnuts at the station
who, shaking his penis at me, screamed
What are you looking at, witch?

Solomon's Seal

I am repotting in the front garden –
Polygonatum multiflorum, aka St Mary's Seal,
aka Sigillum Sanctae Mariae of the Lily family
which bears drooping tubular white flowers
in the axils of its broad sessile leaves.

I am dreaming its promise this autumn
of next summer's green wave
that will break over my ageing body.

A balm, a respite, this afternoon of
woodsmoke and drizzle and the days drawing in.

Then a crucible of restlessness suddenly:
should I leave this city which will kill me with grief?
Something stirring in the blood, under the skin:
will I still live in this suburban estate
when the mystery of the seal breaks open

in the secret petals nestled under leaves,
their delicate sigil unregarded
in the sun pushing northward into my next summer?

Sweeping the Garden

What ya doin? Can I help ya? and there's
Bridie bursting with her news, her weather,
her cousins and aunts and uncles, her tribe,
her songs made up off the top of her head,
her stories, her notions, her deep mnemonics,
her cultured beautiful mind.

She's settled now a year in this estate,
come in off the road to live in a house,
traveller still, forever gypsy,
going to the local primary school, fighting her corner
in the politics of the street, and what it is
to be a girl of nine.
                              I help, or indeed hinder,
sometimes with her homework.
She swims in the oral: looking into a written sentence
is like looking into a bush. Numbers
are blackbirds that all flap up together from the page.

Her teacher has given her a homework journal,
standard issue for the school but a year out of date.
Why would a teacher give a child a blunt tool?

I explain that the days of the week and the dates
of those days are all a year behind so
she'll have to adjust each and every day and numeral
of each and every long-drawn
incarcerated moment of her school year.

As if she hasn't enough on her plate.

'Ha!' she says. 'I get it.
I'm living in the past!'

And merriment opens her face
like a flower. And breaks my heart.

Common Sense

A murmuration of starlings in a rowan tree
mid-August berry feast
and berries raining down upon my head.

The music of what happens is
the sudden siren on the Coast Road
where the boy racer has hit the wall –
Coked up to the gills, says the cop –

and the brakes of the train pulling
into Bayside Station.
               I'm walking the dog
by the dying grove of young chestnuts
where last year, maybe as a sideline
to gathering conkers, children did
methodically strip each chestnut of its bark.

I wanted to wrap the trees in woolly jumpers –
those saplings shivering through the winter.
I watched them fail to bud and fail to leaf.

I watched them die through fair weather
through foul I have watched them die.
My beloved young chestnut grove.
And now an autumn without conkers!

We don't deserve this earth I sometimes think
and yet the children acted from ignorance.
I saw them at it: their rapt gazes as they stript
might have lent a Renaissance artist faces for an altarpiece.

Common sense dictates there'll be bad luck
in store for them down their roads,
in dowry or in handsel they will fail
as the ballad has it.

               Nor would I wish to deal
the hand they have to play
or play it with them.

Hectic

Walking the estuary today, Paula McCarthy,
passing the channel where I'd poured your ashes.
The two breasts of Howth beyond
to nestle your poor head against, my thought
five years ago, demented with grief.

I think of the scouring power of fire
in this the fire season, and of our last talk.
You were helping me move snails
from their lurking hides under the creeper
where they could nip (insofar as snails nip)
out in forays against my seedlings.

You asked about fire in Buddhism and what
it meant – you recalled a photo of a monk
burning in protest at the war.
Was there a Buddhist hell?

Only now. And now. And now – I joked.
And you laughed de profundis.
I don't remember what I said
But seriously ... some guff no doubt or
blah blah blah the way I do go on.

This autumn with the trees hectic in the woods
I'll let you drop leaf by leaf into the void,
let you leave drop by drop in the rain showers
let my love for you flower
in the far off fireworks of the city
as I lay my own demented head
on the two dun breasts of the hill of Howth to hear
as Yeats himself was wont to do when young
the eternal heartbeat of the mother.

We'll never know now what prompted you to use fire
and how much three weeks on Seroxat played its part.
Ourselves, we said, if come to that sad strait would
take some pills or score something lethal on the street

from Homer or Homeboy or whatyoumaycallhim
and nod off forever. As if one had a choice
in the matter. No matter. We go on.

Foot before foot slog up the path.
O volcanic sister, O magma of sorrow,
O roman candle, O meteorite shower,
O heavenly comet, O cut diamond,
O glint and gleam and shine,
Spark my obdurate heart.

The First Day of Winter

My head in the clouds
in the bowl of Akiko's
mother's white miso.

Single Room with Bath, Edinburgh

I slept last night in a room where someone died;
a narrow bed with polycotton sheets,
a window over wet deserted streets,
a tarnished mirror where my face was pied

and strange to me. I tossed, I turned; cold sweats
then prickly heat. I froze, I burned. I fell
into a dream that wasn't mine, some hell
hole, a smell of ether, legs open and wet

with blood. My own? Or the aborted near term child?
I could not tell. I felt my spirit ebb
and drift from me. For certain I was taking my last breath.

I heard a creature cry: part human, part wild.
It brought me to my senses, woke me to the web
of stars outside, refugee from someone else's death.

From Source to Sea

The light makes a river of the scars on your back.
I trace it from source to sea. It spills
off my page into silence, from the mouth into salt bitterness
of tears, beyond comfort of song or poem.

The light makes a river of the scars on your back.
I trace its course from neck to hip, its silken touch,
its pearly loveliness, its dream of shallows,
its song of pools, its memory of curlew
and nightingale, of heron and grebe.

The light makes a river of the scars on your back.
I walk the banks and pick for your pleasure
a posy of wildflowers, the smell of their names,
angelica, chamomile, calendula, dear vulneraries
with their balms and their powers, their beautiful petals
to soothe and to rescue, to help with the pain.

I trace the river the length of your back
to its source – a room, a house, a street
not unlike this one. A man is closing
the shutters on the light of morning. The same
light everywhere we rise to and greet.
He unbuttons his cuffs and rolls up his sleeves.
He is ready for work. So much to be done.

Zealot

There you go rushing for the bus
over the body of your wounded brother,
your broken sister, your lover
who is packing a small bag;

there you go to the meeting,
papers flapping, motions humming in your head;
your bloody footprint:

all that's left
in the aftermath.

Etch

i.m. Osip Mandelstam

What was not committed to birch bark
was scribed in the memory of the hushed zeks
who took Osip's poem to heart.

His poem I write in my own breath
on the windowpane, the dear Irish rain
falling to the garden's purple vetch.

I'll spill acid on this plate
and fetch from deepest darkest shade
the lines that scarred the prisoner's face;

the light that struck in that most wretched place –
the wolves' tracking howl,
the birches singing out the forest's fate.

Flight JIK Olympic Airlines 016 to Ikaria, Greece

The plane judders on final approach: I think there's something
wrong –
only the kick of katabatic wind off the mountain. I've understood
nothing of the air hostess' tense preamble, place
all my faith in one-breath meditation till we are landed and taxiing
along
the runway, plane and shadow joined at last. I step into the waiting
scent of wild thyme and baking earth which must be
what the boy Icarus smelt as he fell, not plunging, but skating
the thermals down. The cypress and the piney wood,
the holm oaks – smudge of green beyond Chrysostomos, the
colour he forgot
in his blue rapture of sky and Aegean when he set course
for the searing heart of the sun. The exact spot
of his burial is disputed. The way of myth to give a carthorse
wings and call it Pegasus; the way of myth to turn a maid into a tree

has brought me here to see where the story ends – away
from the toxic island of my birth, its slings and arrows, that I may
understand the nature of my failure. To hear clearly the father's cry
over the drowned body of his son, in the ancient light that shone
on the bronze-workers at their cire-perdue, their leathers green
from the copper smelt, their nifty casting seen
in the elegant lineaments of the myth. I scan the sky
for rain. The craft fails me: this contraption fails. I move on.

Troika

1 How I Discovered Rhyme

Not long back from London
my father had done a deal with a man
key money down on a house
in Bargy Road, East Wall,
an illegal Corporation tenancy
in those days of no work, no roof,
no hope, no time like the present
to come home with three small children
and another on the way to what

was familiar at least. Dublin rain
and Dublin roads and Dublin streets
and Dublin pubs and Dublin pain.
Mayblossom in the park and empty pockets.

I think it was then my mother gave up:
pre-natal, post-natal who knows now.
They are so young, my mother and father,
to me who has grown old

in their light, in their shade.
They have too much on their plate –
including Ucker Hyland's chickens.
Part of the deal for the house
was to mind this man's chickens.
He kept them in the back yard
in makeshift crates and lofts.
Sporadically he'd deliver sacks of feed.
We'd have pots of popcorn every night
to *Felix the Cat* and to *Bolek and Lolek*
and the birthpangs of Irish Television.

We settled in. We fed the hens.
The man came. He took the eggs.
He'd wring the odd neck.
He wore two overcoats
belted by a length of rope.
And then a letter: the Eviction Notice.
Some neighbour had ratted us out.
There were rows, recriminations,
slammed doors, my father silent.

The stay in Bargy Road ended
on a bitter winter's day,
the Tolka low and the tang of rot.
We came home from school to bailiffs
boarding up the windows, to all
we had on show in the garden,
paltry in the dying light –
a few sticks of furniture,
the mattress with its shaming stain
nearly the shape of Ireland,
the Slot TV, our clothes in pillowcases
and our Christmas dolls grubby
and inadequate on the grass.

My mother was frantically chasing the chickens;
we put down our satchels and joined in.
My father was gone for the lend
of a van or a cart. The streetlights
came on and here comes
the henman around the corner –

Ucker Hyland! Ucker Hyland! –
coats flapping and oaths spitting from his big lips
and all of us then round and round the garden
the winter stars come out and
feathers like some angelic benison
settling kindly on all that we owned.

Why my maternal, and much feared, uncle should visit
me now is a mystery. Both he and my mother dead,
me alone on the side of a mountain in Ikaria
a sanctuary sacred to a god of healing, Asklepius.

I was gathering herbs all morning, then sat
gazing out to sea in a half dream.
Hot springs with a sulphurous whiff,
the rocks around them a deep orange,
roil into the sea in a wraith of steam.

He comes *as large as life and twice as ugly.*
I put him down here in the hope he'll leave me be:
I must have brought him with me, packed
in my rucksack with Robert Graves' *The Greek Myths.*

★

I'm thirteen: my mother is sending me across the city
with Christmas presents for his children,
(all nine daughters – two sons he has yet to sire,
the only reason, he says, he has all those daughters,
trying for boys!)
                          I've to get
two buses with my parcels and the few bob for his wife,
a dark beauty with sad eyes and many tired sighs.
We wouldn't have had that much ourselves
and I'm not to tell my father who's barred him
from the house, barred all mention of his name,
the way he'd turn up drunk and roaring.
We'd be under the covers shaking
or slipping out the back way to avoid him,
the way he'd pull our panties or pyjamas down
and spit on our bottoms and rub the spit in.

Such a strange thing to do. I'll never fathom it.
I ask again what he meant by it in the shade
of this myrtle, in the thyme laden air
the salt taste of my own skin on my tongue.

Their house is a wreck when I get there –
windows smashed and boarded up.
Not a stick of furniture: orange crates to sit on
and jam jars for cups. So many children
with her beautiful eyes.
                              I'm queasy
in my brand new Christmas coat,
patterned with blue and green chevrons,
the first I've ever chosen for myself.
I want to leave that dark house
and run through that new estate
despite my squeaky shiny pinching shoes
to the bus and the city and the river and home.

I wonder even then how it all came to this:
when he arrives in spruced and groomed
in a mohair suit, rolling a fat cigar between thumb
and forefinger. The radio is playing Dickie Rock
or some similar contemporary pop.
We don't want to listen to this muck, he snaps it off
and takes me to the parlour which he keeps locked.
The only key.

                   Inside it's like a babby house
as the old ones used to say. All spic and span.
Carpeted. A three piece suite. A record player
long and slim, reminds me of a coffin
I saw a schoolmate laid out in.
And there in a cage a singing bird –
a canary by name Caruso. He takes him out
gently on a finger and strokes his yellow feathers.
He tells me he loves classical music
and he'll give me a fiver if I can name a classical composer.
I can and I don't. Nobody understands him
he tells me, especially not that cunt out there.
He smells of aftershave and stands too close to me.
He calls my mother a cunt too
and my father an ignorant fucker.

After nine daughters he got the sons he wanted.

His daughters grew to womanhood:
they taught their mother barring orders and legal separation.
They taught their mother the beautiful shining world
of work and peace and dignity and choice.
They taught their mother the new facts of life.

He outlived my own mother by thirty years.
He died alone one Christmas in a city centre flat.
His body lay there for days.

★

I lay him down now in the shade of a holm oak,
partridges chattering, late bees sipping still
at the wild mountain flowers. The sun is falling
behind the mountain, the Aegean turns blood red
for a moment, then fades to a pewter distance.
The moon is nearly full, stars are coming out
slowly, one by one, until the sky is a net
to catch me as I fall and fall and fall
further, willingly into its depths.

3   This Is Not a Confessional Poem

I write it in the light of ancient Greece
or in the ancient light of this mountain.
I write it in the shadow of the myths
or in the shadow of the people who made them.
I do not know that I've the right to say such things.
I only know I must.

I found her in the cold light of Finglas,
my mother curled to a foetal question
in the backyard. The stars were glittering
eyes in the night. The grass was rimed with frost
and crunched underfoot.
                         I remember
thinking how ill clad she was
for the night that was in it.

78

Her brushed nylon pyjamas, her thin bare feet.
Ill shod. Not a sound to be heard
in the sleeping estate. Far off a dog.
Then another. A car starting up,
the engine having trouble catching.

I had woken from a dream of summer,
my first lover, to shouts and doors banging.
I had woken to my father calling out
my mother's name. Again and again.
And *dear sweet jesus* and *o christ*.

The downstairs windows were all open wide.
It brought the frosty air inside.
You could still smell gas.

I found her with her head in the oven.
I dragged her outside. Was all he said
then, and ever after. As if to allay accusation
or set his own story straight, or give the only facts
worth recording. He was not a man for elaborations.
Stoic? Or cynic? To this day I'm still in doubt.
Laconic for sure: though far from Ancient Sparta
he was reared, he would have fitted in.

We thought she was dead.
Her feet were like ice in my hands. Were
it not for the night that was in it
we might have missed her breath –
the thin reed of it rising, her sad tune to the air
proof positive she was still there.

We carried her in between us,
my father and I, never again that close,
or complicit. Never again the same as we were.

The doctor when she came was drunk
and worse than useless. Prescribed more
sleepers and downers, pocketed her fee
and stumbled towards her car.

The sun was coming up, the children
were whingeing for their breakfasts.
The older ones were rushing off to school.

And that is how I leave them now:
I pull the door behind me firmly closed.
The past is a lonely country.
There are no charts, no maps.
All you read is hearsay, as remote
as the myths of this Greek island
where one small boat putters out to sea
in a blaze of morning sunlight
dragging my attention in its wake.

Pangur Bán Reincarnate

on the edge
of this Greek village

as a feral ball
of suspicion and tat;

every morning while I write
out of the May glare

she hunts lizards in the sun
and brings them one by one

to kill them at my feet
before eating them

belly first then head
to twitching tip of tail

except for their shiny teeth.
There's only her and me

this end of Therma,
an out of season spa,

both hunters by trade
though she's much better at it.

St John and My Grandmother – An Ode

I am gazing out at Patmos where St John
received the Book of the Apocalypse.
Some mornings it is on the horizon
very like the name the locals give it
boat of stone. Some mornings
you might see the monastery – a smudge
of white above the rock below the green
luxury of what shade there is, what shade
I imagine.
          More often it is hidden in a haze,
a rumour. What frightens me more
than his vision of the last days is the use
to which the holy book is put –
not content with its true worth, hallucinatory
dreamscape of the eternal now,
a highly polished mirror for the present times.
It's called the Word of God and that means trouble
for people like me. Always has. Always will.

It brings to mind my mother's mother Mary
who'd not an evangelical bone in her entire body,
loving, as she did, the way the earth was made.
All she asked was a decent crop of lilac
and roses coming in when the lilac would fade.
To call her simple is to miss the point
entirely. Avatar of hearth mysteries,
true daughter of the moon, the shining one,
before she'd open the curtains of morning
whether winter or summer while the kettle boiled
she'd tell her dreams to her gathered daughters,
as apocalyptic in their cast as were St John's.
She knew who died in the night,
who'd lose, who'd have a child.
The world was always signal portent,
every single thing stood for something else.
Her dreams, though I was not supposed to hear them,
could rivet, terrorise, warn or shrive you.

Her dreams were instruments of torture
for miscreant daughters who were out of line.
Her dream tongue my first access to poetry:
by her unwritten book I've lived, I'll die.
Here for instance is a dream she had of Marie
a younger daughter gone at seventeen
to work in 1950s London, a scene
my grandmother can only imagine, having
never left Dublin: *Well, I got the boat*
to Holyhead and then the train to Euston.
The tube then, the Northern Line
and there was not a sinner on it
but me and the driver, a blackman.
I got off at Angel, and came up to the street.
It was deserted. Not a sound but dead leaves
underfoot as if it was autumn. Brown
and gold and yellow and blood red the leaves
all the way to Marie's. I came to her door.
It was wide open. Marie, I called. Then louder,
Marie, Marie. Not a sound. I went in the door.
The house was all leaves underfoot,
all the way up the stairs. They were up to my knees.
Her bedroom door was open. I went inside.
Leaves up to my knees. I pushed across to her wardrobe.
I pulled the door open and what was before me
only Marie chopped in a hundred pieces, hacked to death.
And a river of blood came out of the wardrobe,
swept me in a wave right down the stairs
and out the front door onto the empty street.
Not a sound. Not a sinner.
Just leaves and blood. Leaves and blood.

I sometimes tell this dream to my students
though it refuses a didactic read.
If they ask me where my poems come from
it's as good a place as any to begin:
Mary McCarthy's dream songs for her daughters,
as apocalyptic as the visions of St John.
I heard them first before the age of reason.
They've stayed with me word for word

across half a century. I write one down now
in sight of Patmos, the island moving
like a trireme from me further into the haze
from which they both have come –
Mary McCarthy and the Evangelist John.

Hearth Lesson

Either phrase will bring it back –
money to burn, burning a hole in your pocket.

I am crouched by the fire
in the flat in Séan MacDermott Street
while Zeus and Hera battle it out:

for his every thunderbolt
she had the killing glance;
she'll see his fancyman
and raise him the Cosmo Snooker Hall;
he'll see her 'the only way you get any
attention around here is if you neigh';
he'll raise her airs and graces
or the mental state of her siblings,
every last one of them.

I'm net, umpire, and court; most balls
are lobbed over my head.
Even then I can judge it's better
than brooding and silence and the particular hell of the unsaid,
of 'tell your mother…' 'ask your father…'.

Even then I can tell it was money,
the lack of it day after day,
at the root of the bitter words
but nothing prepared us one teatime
when he handed up his wages.

She straightened each rumpled pound note, then
a weariness come suddenly over her,
she threw the lot in the fire.

The flames were blue and pink and green,
a marvellous sight, an alchemical scene.

'It's not enough,' she stated simply.
And we all knew it wasn't.

The flames sheered from cinder to chimney breast
like trapped exotic birds;
the shadows jumped floor to ceiling, and she'd
had the last, the astonishing, word.

The Mushroom Field

at the edge of the estate is gone now,
where I walked so many mornings
with my father before breakfast
in the autumn mist that wreathed the hawthorn

— That one morning when it started snowing
and we looked back at the tracks we had made.

I can hear them sizzling in the pan with butter
I can smell their otherworldly disdain,
and how they came on again and again.

I remember most the silence on those walks,
both of us lonely, both of us in pain.

There's a ten storey apartment block
and a shopping centre going in
over the traces of our footsteps,

the vestiges I lay down on this page
side by side, in the same rhythm, now;
making a path through autumn rain.

Archive

It is only when my father takes bad after Christmas
that we make the effort to get into his room.

It feels intrusive and yet it must be done
as delicately as we can we tiptoe round it.

With the sorting comes the weary recognition
that after this small room the earth shall claim him.

I sit amongst his things in the wintry sunlight
dusting, washing, swabbing down and with a shock

I recognise my younger rounder hand there
in sheaves of notes in tattered folders.

I turn a page and am restored to a Trinity classroom:
W.B. Stanford and the Roots of Greek Drama,

Dionysus and Beatlemania – an aside,
The Peloponnesian War, Pericles, the Athenian Fleet,

The Cynics, Stoics, Tyrants,
The Republic and Hesiod's *Works and Days.*

It's all I have to hold of my ancient confusions.
So much scattered in the squats and flats,

the vagaries of the road, the to's and fro's,
the wasted boys, those seasons down in hell.

There amongst my father's privacies
I forgive myself for the daughter I wasn't.

My Senior Freshman notes he deemed worth saving,
he who never spared a word of praise

or found a language of devotion except for horses.

My Brother Becomes a Man

on a particular October day. After the knock
on the door, after the first reports on the news.

I was in the kitchen in Eslin making bread
watching dough prove, stoking the range

listening to the same reports, oblivious;
thinking god help her she must have been

demented she must have been out of her mind.
The pictures in my head: a woman,

the seafront at Bray, a laneway, a hatchet, a child dead.
Never connecting. Never connecting to us.

When trouble comes to your door he
doesn't knock and he doesn't wipe his feet —

rugpulled tonofbricks punchinthegut no.
None of us were ever the same again.

But my brother who went to the morgue
and who gave the child back his name

who claimed him as one of our kin,
who placed him on the record of the State,

footnote to the times we are living in
as well as private pain, private fate,

my brother becomes a man there where he gazed
on the boy's dead face, when he took the image within

like a holy gift, an icon blazed in gold,
when he assumed the truth of the child's young soul

and shouldered it like the one true cross
and, man that he has become,

in silence he carries the weight and soldiers on.

At Shelling Hill

for Ciarán Carson

*Its arc shaped embankments with its prolific natural vegetation offers cover to the
secretive, comfort and protection to the lazy, and a playground to children*
www.blueflag.org/blueflag/2006/Ireland/Border/Shellinghill

That summer we took the children off on a whim,
a refurbished house at the end of a bumpy lane,
all mod cons and filled with sea light, perched
between coastal meadow and a drop to shingle beach.
Cold for July and very like a rerun of our own childhood –
no car and a three mile walk to the nearest shop.
And time enough to lose track of time, to skim
flat stones and count the skips they made on the plane
of the water; or follow the children as they searched
rock pools for starfish and crabs, keeping them in reach.
The tide pulled them out, and then it would
push them back to us again, like a giant mop,

to where we'd wait to scrutinise their spoils.
The dog nosed rocks and worried dunlin and gull,
collie genes coming out when she herded the tawny heifers
we told the children were the great great great
great great great granddaughters of the brown bull
of Cooley. We played at Cú Chulainn on the strand
dressed in flotsam the tide washed in: fishing net, coils
of trawler rope, a broken float, a scrap of tarp pulled
to shape a warrior's cloak, styrofoam shields, wooden spears;
and when they grew fractious and began to really fight
as night came on or the day turned wet and dull
we'd light a fire, we'd conjure Scáthach, warp spasm, the red hand.

Sometimes I'd walk off alone up Shelling Hill
to muse on how the earth gives back at last
all that circumstance or happenstance would conceal:
grave goods, those offerings to help the dead cross over,
torcs, eagle bones, beads of amber, arrowheads of flint.

Simple things made complex by time. Or complex things simplified.
That woman's body found by a father out with his son. Killed
by a bullet to the back of the head over thirty years past,
restored to her family, to the State's record, a civil burial
in the clear light of day. Here where she was laid bare
of her humble shroud of bramble and scutch, here where a glint
on the dune draws a kestrel to drop, here where played

out again and again covert manoeuvres of that savage war
finally dwindled to a woman's outstretched arms – *I entreat thee ...*
Jean McConville, widow, disappeared mother of ten.
We say nothing to the children about her. Safer the ancient lore.
We show them rainbows in a harrowed field, a magic cauldron
where the rainbow ends, brought back from the shadowy city,
Dun Sceith, the city of the dead. Safer the aboriginal gore.
No mention of Divis, her children left cold and hungry.
Of the spooks who ran her, those who sanctioned her execution,
who bundled her into a car, who executed the order,
who cleaned up after, who dug the hole to put her body in –
which of these is it hardest to pity?

The children loved to watch the hares at play
in the meadow; mornings they loved to track moonshaped
hoofprints along the wet strand. I'd tell them
it's a night-mare, a star horse, with a star blaze
on her forehead. Seals barked from the rocks
and the dog barked back. *Long long ago a she-seal*
came ashore to gather sea shells ... They'd
pick the earliest blackberries, they'd traipse
with purple lips across freshwater streams, the hems
of their jeans soaked, they'd come home in a daze,
minnows in their buckets, knees scraped, hair tossed, socks
lost, to tumble into bed. Later we'd kneel

and tuck their tangled limbs under the duvet.
Soon enough to be doing with history, to be doing with truth.
Deep, and deeper, they'd sleep in the ceaseless lull of the tide
and truth was that full moon rising on the water,
the O of its becoming taking our breath away.
Come Sunday, before we left, we picked flowers,

armfuls of meadowsweet, cranesbill, vetch, an array
of lupin, of the wild dog rose, and walked to where Bláthnat,
or so we've told them, she who was lover of Cú Chulainn, is buried.
Lady-made-of-flowers, surprising us, they called her,
cross-connecting from what Gaelic they can yet say.
So to the children the last word, her requiem prayer:

Lady made of flowers, bride of the earth, rest in peace.

The Wolf Tree

for Margaret Dorgan

To see the wolf tree is a skill best learnt the hard way.
Or the easy way. So much depends on stillness.
Just look into the woods for as long as it takes:
the wolf tree is the one with laterals,
branches growing out and sideways from the bole.
You'll scan and scan and scan and fear
you can't find the tree for the woods
until the moment when your attention snags – a disruption
in patterning: horizontals suddenly when all around
are verticals. Once you find your first wolf tree
your vision will be sharper for the next, which may
also be hard to find. But never as hard as the first.

The wolf tree remembers when it was the only tree
in an open field. It remembers when
there was no competition for the light.
Because it had the field to itself it could be itself
in the wind and the rain and the blessed sun.
It is a kind of alpha tree, with a kind of alpha memory.

The trees that subsequently take root
from mast or nut or seed, windborne
or carried on an animal's flank or shat down by birds,
these race towards the light and fight for it;
they reach straight upwards and mask the wolf tree
eventually, from all but the keenest loneliest eyes.

If you were to dream back through all the trees
in all the forests the earth has grown,
to the oldest, the original tree, the archeopteris, say,
believed from a spore engendered,
and climb up through its ferny branches –
imagine the field you might survey,
imagine the vista that might unfold,
before the wolf tree's unleaving,

like the hours of your life,
finds you shivering, naked, unmasked and old:
revealed out in your own original domain
the desert sand moving towards you
the pressure mounting, the original diamond pain.

Coda: Payne's Grey

I am trying to paint rain

day after day
I go out into it

drizzle, shower, downpour

but not yet the exact
spring rain

warm and heavy and slow

each drop
distinct & perfect

that I wait for

by this water's edge
where some leaf of memory

will come down with the flood

the river in spate
broadening out to the sea.

Acknowledgements

My thanks to the editors, producers, curators of the following:

80 mph: A Festschrift for Leland Bardwell, ed. Nicholas McLachlan; 80mph Press, Dublin, 2002

A Fine Statement: An Irish Poets' Anthology, ed. John McDonagh; Poolbeg, Dublin, 2008

Amnesty Ireland

Answering Back, ed. Carol Ann Duffy; Picador, London, 2007

Art of Friendship 2005

Best of Irish Poetry 2008 Scoth na hÉigse, ed. Thomas McCarthy and Bríd Ní Mhóráin; Southword Editions, the Munster Literature Centre, Cork, 2007

Best of Irish Poetry 2009 Scoth na hÉigse, ed. Paul Perry and Nuala Ni Chonchúir; Southword Editions, the Munster Literature Centre, Cork, 2008

Bloomsday Magazine 2003

Brass on Bronze: Errigal Writers 2005; Errigal Press, Donegal, 2005

Canadian Journal of Irish Studies

Citywide

The Clifden Anthology 2003, 2004, 2007, ed. Brendan Flynn; Clifden Community Arts Week, Galway

A Conversation Piece, ed. Adrian Rice and Angela Reid; Ulster Museum in association with Abbey Press, Belfast, 2002

The Graphic Studio

The Irish Times

Japan Journal of Irish Studies

Metre

Migrating Minds I & II

The Music of Words, RTE Radio 1

Our Shared Japan, ed. Irene De Angelis and Joseph Woods; The Dedalus Press, Dublin, 2007

Out of Fashion, ed. Carol Ann Duffy; Faber & Faber, London, 2004

Oxfam Calendar 2006

PN Review

Poems & Pastries

poetryinternational.org, December 2005

Ringsend Action Project, Christmas Card 2003
The Sailor and the North Star (with translations into Japanese by
   Nobuaki Tochigi); Nobi Press, Tokyo, 2006
The Stinging Fly
The Stony Thursday Book
Tratti
An Sionnach
A Wag on the Wa Side
With love from me to you, BBC 4
World Literature Today
The Yellow Nib

My gratitude to the staff, students, and surrounding community, of
St Patrick's College and Dublin City University, where I was Poet-
in-Residence during 2007, a position that allowed me time to
complete this collection.

My thanks to Veronica Bolay and Mayo County Council Libraries for
use of the cover image. And thanks too to Frank O'Reilly and Austin
Vaughan for their help.

Notes

Sea was published in a fine art edition edited by Thomas Dillon Redshaw and designed by Paulette Myers-Rich; Traffic Street Press in association with the Centre for Irish Studies, St Paul, Minnesota, March 2007.

'From Source to Sea' was commissioned by Amnesty Ireland to mark the commencement of their campaign *Take a Step to Stamp Out Torture*, 2002 to 2004.

'A Change of Life' sequence and 'Teaching "Kubla Khan" to the FÁS Trainees at the Recovery through Art, Drama, and Education Project' were included in *Days Like These*, Brooding Heron Press, Washington State, 2007. Fine art edition, editing and design by Sam and Sally Green.

'Her Void: A Cemetery Poem' was commissioned by Evan Chambers for the music/song cycle *The Old Burying Ground*, 2007.

Six Sycamores was published by Crowquill Press, Belfast, 2004, with drawings by Marie Foley, book designed and edited by Julian Watson. Poems commissioned under the Per Cent for Art Scheme by the Office of Public Works on the occasion of the opening of the Link Building between number 51, (at one stage the Museum of Industry), and number 52, (built in 1771 by the banker David La Touche) on the east side of St Stephen's Green, Dublin, in 2001.